BLS WORKING PAPERS

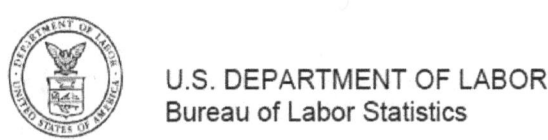 U.S. DEPARTMENT OF LABOR
Bureau of Labor Statistics

OFFICE OF PRICES AND LIVING
CONDITIONS

The Used Car Price Index: A Checkup and Suggested Repairs

B. Peter Pashigian, University of Chicago

Working Paper 338
March 2001

The views expressed are those of the author and do not necessarily reflect the policies of the U.S. Bureau of Labor Statistics or the views of other staff members.   This paper was part of the U.S. Bureau of Labor Statistics Conference on *Issues in Measuring Price Change and Consumption* in Washington, DC, June 2000.

The Used Car Price Index: A Checkup and Suggested Repairs

by

B. Peter Pashigian
Graduate School of Business
University of Chicago

Paper presented at Conference on "Issues in Measuring Price Change & Consumption," sponsored by the Bureau of Labor Statistics, Department of Labor, June 5 - 8

NB. Professor Pashigian passed away on October 18, 2000. This was the last version of the paper received from him.

Introduction

The Bureau of Labor Statistics (BLS) has published the used car price index since December 1952 as part of the Consumer Price Index (CPI). As its 48th birthday approaches, the used car price index merits a timely review for at least two reasons. First, compared to the new car price index, the used car price index is akin to an ignored stepchild, receiving less scrutiny but deserving of more attention. Second, there are nagging doubts and misgivings within the BLS about accuracy of the used car price index. These doubts arise from the suspect time series behavior of the used car index, related in part to the "higher" mean growth rate but especially to the "excess" volatility of the used car price index. Possible underlying causes of this questionable behavior are numerous. Some candidates come to mine. The questionable behavior of the used car price index could be an undesirable byproduct of the sampling procedures adopted by the BLS. Or, could the source of the price information that the BLS relies on be the culprit? What role has the treatment of quality improvements played in explaining the suspect behavior of the used car price index? While any or all of these could be the underlying causes of the questionable behavior and should not be slighted, could the observed "excess" volatility of the used car price index be a real phenomenon? Used car markets might have less elastic supply curves and experience larger demand shocks compared to those observed in the new car and other durable good markets. This alliance of a less elastic supply curve and larger demand shocks could explain the observed "excess" volatility of used car prices.

The paper opens with a brief history of the used car price index. Section II establishes some basic facts about the used car price index. How fast has the used car price index grown over time and how volatile has the index been? Because there is no obvious way to assess volatility on an absolute scale, used car price volatility must be judged on a comparative basis. Since the used and new car markets are interrelated, a natural comparison is between the mean growth rate and volatility of the used car price index with that of the new car price index and also with price indices for other products known for their volatility. Section II presents some answers to these questions.

A comprehensive review of the used car price index inevitably involves an examination of the procedures adopted by the BLS for selecting a sample of used cars and how those procedures have changed over time. The sample selection methods adopted for used cars can be compared to the procedures followed for other durable goods for consistency of practice. How closely does the BLS sample of used cars mimic the new cars that were sold in recent years? If large discrepancies are discovered, what are the causes and consequences of these discrepancies on the behavior of the used car price index? These issues are discussed in sections III and IV.

In Section V attention is directed at the feasibility of using other secondary sources of used car price information. Several commercial guides publish used car price information. The results of a previous study that used secondary source for price information are reviewed. Instead of relying on auction price data, as collected and published by the National Automobile Dealers Association (NADA), the BLS could rely on other secondary sources of used car price information to construct its used car price index. If such a change was made, how would the mean growth rate and the volatility of the used car price index change? A preliminary but detailed exploration of comparative volatility of different price sources is presented in the last section of this paper where the currently used National Automobile Dealers Association auction prices are compared with prices published in Kelley's Blue Book. Hopefully, this preliminary pilot project will shed light on whether volatility of the used car prices would be lower if the BLS used a different secondary data source. Finally, in making adjustments to used car prices because of quality change, the BLS assumes that its measure of the percentage quality improvement (obtained from auto manufacturers) affects used car prices and has the same percentage effect on the price of a used car as the car ages. The paper ends with tests of these hypotheses.

I. A Brief History of the Used Car Price Index

A brief history of the used car price index is presented for the convenience of a curious reader. The history will be mercifully brief because there is no paper trial that an outside investigator such as myself can follow. The rationales for the numerous decisions that were made sporadically over the years are a part of an undocumented verbal tradition, known only to those who made the decisions but who have since moved on.

The used car price index was introduced into the Consumer Price Index in December of 1952. The details of sample selection in the early years are fuzzy at best. At some point, the used car sample consisted of just 21 models that were from 2 to 6 years so that a total of 105 used cars prices were gathered. The models were selected based on the production totals for the 1970-1974 models years (Kellar). This investigator could not find information that described the procedures used to select models or how prices of those models were collected after the used car index was introduced. Apparently, no one thought it important to adjust used car prices for year to year quality improvements until 1987. As is documented below, this glaring omission had significant repercussions on the behavior of the used car price index from 1953 to 1987.

It was not until the major 1987 revisions were introduced that the BLS made a serious effort to adjust the used car prices for quality improvements. In contrast, the BLS began to make adjustment for quality improvements of new cars in 1967, twenty years earlier. Numerous other changes were introduced to the index in 1987. The sample was expanded significantly. Second, the BLS restricted its attention to only used cars sold by business (rental car agencies, governments, etc.) to consumers. It obtained information about the age and types of cars sold by business to consumers via a report published by a private company. These important decisions had a major impact on what cars were included into the BLS sample and on the behavior of the index. Of the many changes introduced in

1987 one of the more significant is the treatment of quality improvements. For the first time the BLS confronted the quality improvement issue directly. It borrowed the method that it used to adjust new car prices for quality improvements and applied it to used cars as well. As will demonstrated below, some of the odd behavior of the index is due to the tardy introduction of a quality adjustment.

This brief review is neither comprehensive nor definitive. The reader is spared a more detailed description of these changes until later in the paper.

II. Comparative Mean Growth and Volatility of Used Car Prices

A. Annual Percentage Price Change:

This section presents summary statistics on the mean growth rate and price volatility for selected products in the Consumer Price Index. Because this study focuses on used cars, the main objective is to establish some facts about the mean growth rate and volatility of used car prices and then to compare used car price behavior to the price behavior of selected components in the CPI. A natural comparison is between used and new cars so throughout this paper the price volatility of used cars will often be compared to new cars. Other useful comparisons are between used cars and products that have been singled out by the BLS for their greater price volatility, such as energy and food, etc.

This examination of the used car price index begins by first looking at the mean growth and volatility of year-to-year price changes in the index and then moves on to examine monthly price data. For most of the studied product groups, the sample of annual observations covers a forty-three year period, beginning in 1955 and continuing through 1998. Over this long period there have been several changes in methodology, data collection methods, weighting procedures, etc. Sometimes, changes in methodology are adopted but a revision is not or cannot be made to previous years of the price series. Consequently, the existing price series are probably not entirely consistent over time. So, our summary measures of price volatility will reflect the effects of these changes as well as the underlying price volatility of the product. The initial year of 1955 is selected because the BLS began to collect transaction versus list prices for new cars in the middle of 1954. To analyze annual price volatility, the price ratio P_t / P_{t-1} is the variable of interest where P_t is the price index in year t and P_{t-1} is the price index in the previous year. The mean, standard deviation and the standard deviation/mean ratio of the P_t/P_{t-1} ratio are calculated for each product.

Table 1 shows the mean M (row 1), standard deviation SD (row 2), the ratio of the standard deviation to the mean, SD/M, (row 3) and the ratio of SD/M for each product relative to the SD/M for used cars (row 4) for 6 product categories: new vehicles, used vehicles, energy, food, the Consumer Price Index (CPI), and CPI excluding energy, food, shelter and used cars. The BLS considers energy and food prices among the more volatile components of the CPI, so much so that the BLS not only reports the CPI but the CPI with the more volatile sectors excluded.

A puzzling, if not disturbing, feature of Table 1 is that from 1955 to 1998 the mean of the used car price ratio exceeds the mean of the new car price ratio by a full 2.1 percentage points per year. Another way of illustrating this odd behavior is to regress the used car price ratio, R_t^u, on the new car price ratio, R_t^n. The estimated equation is

$$R_t^u = .236 + 1.25\, R_t^n$$
$$(.311)\ (.302)$$

where the standard errors are in the brackets below the line. The new and used car price ratios are equal when $R_t^n = .944$. Since the new car price ratios have been invariably greater than one, the regression results indicate that the used car price ratio has exceeded the new car price ratio in most years.

Just how could the used car price ratio consistently exceed the new car price ratio? The higher mean price ratio for used car prices displayed in row 1 is puzzling for both new and used car prices are suppose to be adjusted for quality change, or so I thought when I began this project. As noted by Gordon (p. 322), a difference in the mean price ratios would lead to the ridiculous conclusion that the used car price would ultimately exceed the new car price. This puzzling difference occurred because the BLS has been more successful and conscientious over time in adjusting new car prices for quality improvements than it has for used car prices. Much to my surprise, I learned that the BLS apparently made no quality adjustment to used cars until 1987. Consequently, the used car price index had an upward drift to it, in part because of the annual quality improvements built into new cars. As documented below, this excessive upward drift has disappeared since 1987 when the BLS faced the quality adjustment issue head-on and began to apply the new car price adjustment for quality change to used cars as well.[i]

A comparison of the first two columns shows that used car prices have been more volatile than new car prices, both absolutely (SD: row 2) and relative to the mean growth rate (SD/M: row 3)) of the price index. Used car prices are less volatile than energy prices, but much of the apparent volatility of energy prices is concentrated in two episodes of rapidly escalating and then contracting crude oil prices. Used car prices are much more volatile than food prices, using either an absolute (SD) or a relative standard (SD/M).

There is some evidence that price volatility has decreased over the forty-three year period, at least for some product groups. Table 2 shows the same data for the 1955 – 1975, (except where otherwise noted) sub-period, the 1976 – 1998 sub-period, and the 1989 –1998 sub-period. Between 1976 and 1998 the volatility of energy prices increased and this contributed to the increased price volatility for the CPI. When the more volatile sectors like energy, housing, food and used cars are excluded, the CPI was less volatile in the second than the first half of the period. While the price volatility of new cars declined in the second period, the decline for used cars was negligible. The decline was larger in both an absolute and a relative sense for new than for used cars (row 4). Again, we find that used car prices increased more rapidly than new car prices, although the difference between the mean growth rates decreased from 2.4 percentage points per year in the first sub-period to 1.8 percentage points per year (row 1) in the second sub-period. This decrease reflects the BLS effort to adjust used car prices for quality improvements in recent years.

To validate this conclusion, an even shorter sub-period, from 1989 to 1998, was examined. The bottom panel of Table 2 shows a tiny difference of only .005 per year between the mean of the price ratios for new and used cars. It appears that the quality adjustment procedure introduced by the BLS after 1987 has effectively eliminated the gap. The difference in the mean price ratios for new and used cars over the 1955 – 1998 span appears to be due in part to the omission of a quality adjustment for used cars in the earlier years of the sample. In passing it is worth emphasizing that between 1989 and 1998 the relative volatility of used cars exceeded that of other products including energy. It is apparent from this brief survey that annual used car prices are relatively more volatile.

This abbreviated history of used and new car price behavior can be instructive. The large difference between the mean price ratio for new and used cars lasts for an extended period of time – apparently between 1955 and 1987 after which an adjustment of quality improvements was adopted. Why it took so long to recognize and account for this difference remains a mystery from this vantagepoint. Used car price ratios cannot be persistently larger than new car price ratios. If they were, lower quality items would ultimately sell for more than higher quality items. The excess between the mean price ratio of used over that of new cars was allowed to persist much too long and should have triggered an alarm that something was wrong with either the new or used or both price indices. Perhaps, a reexamination of the new and used car price indices would have lead to a quicker adoption of a revised price adjustment for quality improvements in used cars.

B. Explanations for the Greater Volatility of Annual Used Car Prices

This review of the cross sectional and times series results has raised two questions. First, why did used car prices growing more rapidly than new car prices? Second, why is volatility greater for used than new cars? As to the first question, a finger has been pointed at an inadequate adjustment for the quality improvement of used relative to new cars up until 1987. The absence of a quality adjustment for used cars explains at least part of the gap.

There are several possible explanations for the greater volatility of used car prices. One possible explanation has to do with the different sources of the price data used to calculate the used and new car price indices. Differences in the collection of used and new car prices may have artificially raised used car price volatility. Later, we try to shed some light on the effects of the sources of data on price volatility.

Another possible explanation is that the observed greater price volatility of used compared to new car prices is real and has little to do with the quality of the underlying price data. It is instructive to use a demand and supply model for new and used cars to explain why used car prices could be more volatile than new car prices. Differences in (1) the supply elasticity of new versus used cars and in (2) the demand variability of new versus used cars could explain the observed differences in price volatility. Over the whole period the correlation between the annual price ratio for new cars and the price ratio of used cars equals 0.3. This positive correlation in annual price changes suggests that increases in the demand for new cars are positively related with the increase in the demand for used cars. However, the size of the correlation between percentage price changes is not large suggesting that there are times when an increase in demand for new cars occurs when the demand for used cars either does not increase or decreases.

If year-to-year percentage shifts in the market demand curve are comparable for used as for new cars, then outward and inward shifts in the market demand curve and a less elastic supply curve for used than for new cars will create greater percentage price changes for used than for new cars. So, one explanation for the greater price volatility of used cars is that the supply elasticity is smaller for used than new cars. The two panels in Figure 1 shows equilibrium prices for three positions of the demand curve for new and used cars. The equilibrium prices for used cars are U_1, U_2 and U_3 while the equilibrium prices for new cars are N_1, N_2, and N_3. If the probability of the demand function shifting from D_i to D_j with i = 1, 2 or 3 and j = 1, 2 or 3 is the same for used as new cars, then the percentage price change will be larger for used than new cars. For example, say the probability of demand shifting from D_1 to D_3 is the same for new and used cars, then the resulting price ratio will be N_3/N_1 for new cars and U_3/U_1 for used cars. Given these assumptions, the standard deviation of the percentage price change will be larger for used rather than new cars. Another implication of the model is that the volatility of used car quantities should be smaller than for new cars. Unfortunately, the absence of used car sales data over an extended period prevents the testing of this implication.

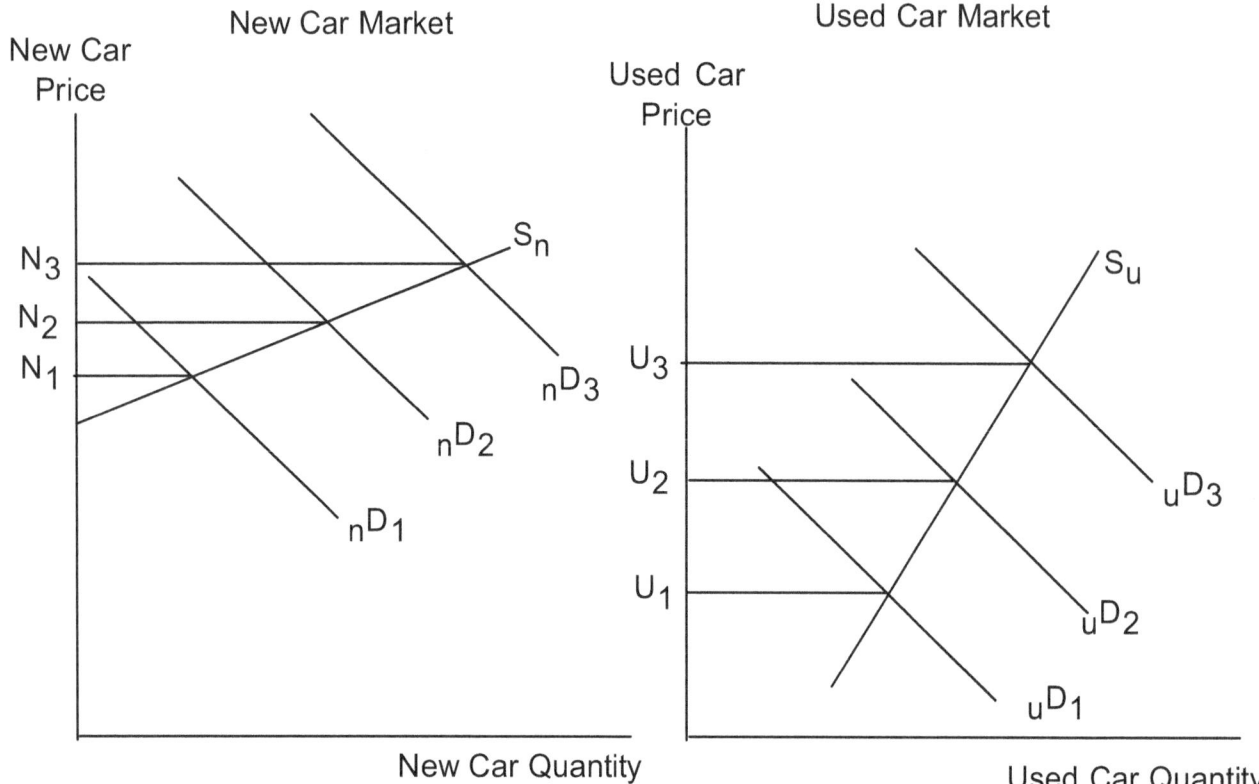

Figure 1: New and Used Car Price Volatility
Caused by Demand Shifts

By a simple extension of this model, the volatility of new car prices would decline over time if the supply elasticity of new cars became still more elastic over time. Another possible explanation for the decline in new car price volatility over time is that the year to year shifts in the position of new car demand curve has become smaller over time. This may have occurred as the relative importance of the annual model change has diminished over time. Either or both changes could explain why new car price volatility has decreased more over time than has used car price volatility.

C. Monthly Price Volatility

Instead of measuring price volatility from year to year, it can be measured from month to month. Part of the within-year variability in prices is due to seasonal factors and part to real factors that create greater monthly price variability. Below we show that used car prices have a larger seasonal swing in prices and, more surprisingly, they are more volatile than the monthly prices of new cars even after adjusting for seasonal swings.

Two measures of monthly price volatility are considered. The first measure is the ratio of the non-seasonally adjusted price to the seasonally adjusted price, NSP_t/SP_t where NSP_t is the non-seasonally adjusted price in month t and SP_t is the seasonally adjusted price in month t. This ratio is the seasonal factor for month t. By how much is the price in month t systematically higher or lower than the average month. The larger the fluctuation of this ratio throughout the calendar year, the more important is the seasonal in prices. The second measure is the monthly percentage change in the seasonally adjusted price index, SMP_t/SMP_{t-1} where SMP_t is the seasonally adjusted price index in month t and SMP_{t-1} is the seasonally adjusted price index in the previous month. The second measure abstracts from the seasonal variation in prices and looks at the remaining monthly price variability.

It is well known that new car prices follow a systematic seasonal pattern. New car prices are typically higher at the beginning of a new model year and lower at the end of the model year. However, this seasonal pattern has been diminishing in importance over time (Pashigian, Bowen and Gould 1995). The fluctuation of prices because of the introduction of new models should play a less important role for used cars if consumers purchase used cars for basic or reliable transportation and place less value on out-of-date fashion features. Nonetheless, Table 3 shows that monthly used car prices fluctuate even more than do new car prices or energy and food prices. As noted above, new car prices fluctuate substantially over the model year. However, the seasonal price variability of used car prices has not been look into before. Apparently, used car prices have an even larger seasonal factor. The new and used car price indexes fluctuate relative more seasonally than do the price indexes for many of the products that make up the index.

Now consider the second measure, monthly fluctuation in seasonally adjusted prices. From 1955 to 1998 ST/M is comparable for new and used cars. Once again, the energy sector has the highest ST/Mean ratio. Caution should be exercised however since the results are sample dependent. The bottom panel of Table 4 shows the monthly volatility results are different for the more recent 1989-1998 sub-period. In recent years monthly used car prices are absolutely and relatively more volatile than new cars. Over the 1989 to 1998 interval the annual or monthly data show that used car prices are more volatile than new car prices. This occurs in spite of the fact that the monthly used car price index is a three-month moving average.

III. A Search for Consistency in the BLS Price Collection Methodology

A. Comparing the Procedure for Housing with Used Cars

The purpose of the CPI is to measure the average price change over time for a given market basket. With a perfect index, the quantity weights of the market basket of goods will reflect the goods purchased by consumers. Ideally, the CPI should measure the required percentage increase or decrease in the expenditure of a representative consumer who bought the CPI market basket brought about by a myriad of individual price changes between any two dates.

The treatment of durable goods in the CPI raises a special and difficult problem. When the price of a non-durable good rises, relative prices change and the consumer is worse off. When the price of a durable good rises, a first time buyer of a used durable good is worse off than if the durable good price had not increased and would require an offsetting cost of living increase so that the consumer could purchase the market basket that would have been purchased had the price not risen. An existing owner of a used durable could be thought of hypothetically selling the used car in the market at a higher price and then buying it back. Because of the price increase, the consumer faces a change in relative prices but receives a capital gain on the sale of the used car. If the consumer owns a two-year-old used car worth $16,000 and its price increases by $1,000, she could hypothetically sell the car at $17,000 and then repurchase it at the higher price because she received a capital gain of $1,000 when she sold the car. So she could continue to purchase the market basket that she had purchased before the price of the durable good increased even though she would not because of the change in relative prices.

If the sole objective of the price index is to measure the average price change of goods over a given time period, then the used car transaction should be treated like a non-durable good transaction and included in the CPI. On the other hand, which prices should be included in the index depends in large part on what the index is to be used for. If the price index is used to derive an estimate of the required income change so that the consumer could buy the same market basket after the price changes, the price change for used car should not be included in calculating the average price change for the index since it would involve double counting. The owner of the durable good has already received a capital gain because of the price increase. So, a further income change is unwarranted to offset the price increase. This reasoning would imply that only those transactions where consumers are first time buyers of a durable should be used to create the weight for the durable good in the CPI. I believe this is the philosophy behind the 1987 adjustments.

The BLS has found it difficult to follow a consistent methodology when pricing the service flows from durable goods in part because of the absence of relevant price data for some durable goods. As a consequence, a consistent treatment of durable goods by the BLS has proven difficult to achieve. Each pricing group appears to develop an independent methodology for collecting price data for each type of durable good. As a consequence, consistency between the adopted methodologies has not had a high priority and has not been achieved.

This is best illustrated by the different treatments the BLS gives to housing, which as of December 1999 represents 39.6 percent of the CPI with shelter representing 30.2 percent, and used cars represents only 1.9 percent. When pricing the services of the housing stock, the BLS currently derives estimates of the owner's rental equivalent of the existing housing stock. Rental equivalence measures the change in the amount that a homeowner would pay to rent, or would earn from renting, his or her home in a competitive market place. Since 1983, the rental equivalence index has been based on the implicit rent of owner units. Until January 1999, these implicit rents were determined by changes in the pure rents of matched rental units. The weight for rental equivalence in the CPI is based on the implicit rents reported by homeowners in a household survey. Changes in the rental equivalence index are determined by changes in the rents of a sample of rental units, weighted to be representative of the owner-occupied housing stock.

If it could be easily implemented, the BLS would like to apply the rental equivalence concept to other durable goods as well. Unfortunately, this has not proved viable because of the difficulty of obtaining appropriate lease data. Hence, the BLS applies a different methodology for other durable goods. For new and used cars, the BLS obtains prices for specified qualities of cars. For new cars it has obtained "market prices" for the purchase of specified new cars. A few years ago it investigated the possibility of using market lease rates for new cars to develop a rental equivalent measure, as used for housing. It did not pursue this avenue because, at the time, the lease market for new cars was just developing and was still too thin. Since then, the leasing market for new cars has expanded rapidly and the BLS has begun experimenting with the rental equivalence concept for leased cars. Applying the rental equivalent concept to used cars, appears less promising at this time. The rental market for used cars is much less well developed so it does not appear as feasible at this time to derive a rental equivalent price index for used cars.

The BLS treats the pricing of used cars differently. In 1987 a major change in the methodology was introduced and a larger sample of cars was selected. At that time the BLS reduced the weight that the used car category was assigned in the CPI from 2.507 to 1.249 percent by limiting used car expenditures to the purchase of used cars by consumers from business, government etc. The sale of a used car from one consumer to another was considered a transfer and not an expenditure (except for dealer profit). The BLS limited its sample of cars from the sales of used cars by non-consumers to consumers, taking account car characteristic such as size of car, body style, engine size, front or rear wheel drive, etc. For most goods, the BLS collects data by returning to the same outlet each month to price the item. The BLS uses a different procedure for used cars. Because it could not assure that it would find the same used car of a given quality month after month at outlets selling used cars, it obtains its used car price data from a national average price that is derived from auction prices at numerous weekly auto auctions. The National Automobile Dealers Association (NADA) reports these prices in their Official Used Car Trade-In Guide. In each year each car included in the sample is between 2 and 6 years old and has a pre-specified set of options.

The decision to use auction prices was a critical one. Not only are auction prices more like wholesale rather than retail prices but the sample of cars that are sold in auctions are hardly a random sample of the population of used cars from two to six years old. As shown below, the sample of auction cars excludes the many popular foreign cars, since few foreign cars are sold as fleet sales. Fewer of the more popular domestic cars are sold as fleet sales as well.

If the same methodology used to derive used car price index was applied to housing, then the price of housing (or the rental equivalent) should be based only on sale prices (or rents paid) for new houses or used homes that were sold by firms and governments since these would business to consumer transactions. Sales of existing used houses by one consumer to another would be considered as transfers within the consumer sector, as are the sales of used cars from one consumer to another. More importantly, this would imply a change in the weight assigned to housing in the CPI. On the other hand, if the methodology adopted for the pricing used housing was followed for used cars, then the sample of used cars should include a random sample of all used car transactions, not only those from business to consumers, as has been followed since 1987. It would seem that a desirable long-term goal is to strive for more consistency in the methodology across products.

IV. The Representativeness of the BLS Sample of Used Cars

A. The BLS Sample of Used Cars Under Samples the Best Selling Cars

Throughout the 1990s the BLS has relied on two different data sources to select a sample of used cars. Between 1990 and 1997, BLS relied on a Rhunzheimer International Survey to draw a sample of used cars sold by rental car agency, governmental units, credit companies etc. to consumers. The Rhunzheimer bi-annual reports showed the number of cars sold by businesses to consumers by age and type of car (body style, options, engine size, front or rear wheel drive, etc.). Because the report was recently terminated, the BLS turned to the Consumer Expenditure Survey (CES) beginning with 1998 to draw a sample of used cars bought by consumers. These two data sources sample a different set of used cars. The Rhunzheimer survey focuses only on the sales of used cars by firms to consumers, and excludes sales from one consumer to another even when an intermediary like a car dealer is used. So the resulting sample will depend on which cars are purchased by businesses for their use. If businesses select cars based on the favorable price that they can get from the car companies, then the more successful cars in the market which are discounted less will not be purchased by rental agencies and governments. Or, businesses might only buy the basic trim line of a model with fewer options. This means that successful cars have a lower probability of showing up in the BLS sample. Imported cars are less likely to show up in the BLS sample.

With the shift to the CES in 1998, the BLS abruptly shelved one of the requirements imposed in the 1987 revisions -- only business to consumer transactions would be eligible for consideration. Beginning in 1998, all used car transactions were now eligible for the purpose of selecting a sample of used cars even though this selection procedure seems inconsistent with the philosophy advanced with the 1987 revisions.

The Consumer Expenditure Survey includes a sample of all used car purchases reported by consumers. In principle it should give a more representative sample of the used cars bought by consumers whether those cars were bought from firms or other consumers. My expectation was to find the popular cars appearing more frequently in the 1998 sample than in the earlier samples.

To determine how representative is the BLS sample of used cars, I compared the frequency with which the cars in the BLS sample were among the top 10 best selling models when new over the previous 6 years. How closely do the cars in the BLS sample mimic the new car sales of the most popular cars during the last six years? If the top ten best selling new cars (ranked by units sold) accounted for (say) 40% of the new car market in the last six years, were 40% of the used cars in the BLS sample among the top ten best selling new cars?

Two cautions deserve mention. To compare the top 10 cars in the last six years against the BLS car sample implicitly assumes that the resale pattern of the top 10 best selling cars is similar to that of used cars in the BLS sample. This is unlikely to be true. The more successful selling cars when new are probably held by the original buyer for more years and traded-in less frequently. While true, this is unlikely to explain the large discrepancy between the top 10 share of the new car market and the share of cars in the BLS sample that were in the top 10. Some preliminary evidence is presented below. Second, the BLS draws its used car sample based on consumer expenditures for used cars and not on units sold. My decision to rely on units sold as a standard was governed by the availability of units sold data.

At the time this analysis was undertaken, the only data set available to me was the so-called "specification or characteristics" data set. This data set shows among other things the auction location and the options on each car included in the sample. The specification data set includes an additional observation for each model that is used to calculate monthly depreciation. In some cases a third observation for the same model will be included when another car must be substituted to calculate depreciation. The 1998 specification data set has 1243 observations which was reduced to 1210 useable observations while the number of observations that the BLS uses to calculate the price index is 563. Roughly speaking, each model is double counted in the "specification" data set. The sensitivity of the results to the size of the sample is not known at this time but I suspect the results will not change appreciably if the smaller sample had been used.

For each calendar year, the top 10 selling models were identified in each of the last 6 years. For example, for 1990 we looked at the 10 best selling new cars in each year from 1985 to 1990, i.e. cars that would be 1 to 6 years old at the end of 1990. For all the one-year old cars in the BLS sample, we determined what fraction of the BLS one-year-old cars were among the top 10 best selling cars when they were new. We repeat this procedure for all used BLS cars for ages from 2 to 6 years old in 1990. Table 5 shows that in 1990 150 of the 746 models in the BLS sample (or 20%) were ranked in the top 10 new cars over the previous six years. In contrast row 5 shows that the top 10 best selling new cars (which includes domestically produced and imported cars) in years 1985 to 1990 accounted for 37% of the total sales of domestic and imported cars. A comparison of rows 3 and 5 shows that in each year the BLS sample of cars under counts the 10 best selling domestically produced and imported cars in the U.S. new car market. The mean percentage of BLS sample of cars that were in the top 10 is 25.9% between 1990 and 1997 while the mean combined market share of the top 10 best selling cars of domestically produced and imported cars was 43.6%, a difference of 17.7 percentage points.

The procedure for calculating the market share of the top 10 best selling cars does not distinguish between cars sold to consumers versus those sold to firms and governments. How the average discrepancy reported above would change if only cars that were sold to consumers could be identified is unclear. However, it likely that the top 10 best selling cars would have a lower probability of being sold to firms and governments. Hence, the market share of the top 10 cars that are sold only to consumers would be still higher. To this extent, our procedure may underestimate the difference.

In general the best selling cars are under-reported in the BLS sample. The mean difference of 17.7 percentage points is a consequence of selecting used cars sold by rental car agencies governmental units and others. Those cars are unrepresentative of the population of used cars held by consumers and may be unrepresentative of all used cars that are sold. Honda Accord and the Toyota Camry were among the best selling new cars in the automobile market throughout the 1990s, as was the Ford Taurus. Yet, they are consistently under represented in the BLS sample throughout the nineties. Makers of these and other best selling cars have less incentive to sell their cars to fleets. If the purpose of the used car price index is to measure the average price change of used car sales, the procedures used to select the sample of cars between 1990 and 1998 should be reviewed both with regard to the criteria for inclusion and for the sample selection methods.

The Consumer Expenditure Survey (CES) reports information about consumer purchases of used cars and (light) trucks. As noted above, the BLS turned to the CES to create the 1998 BLS sample of used cars bought by consumers. Starting in 1998, the BLS expanded the sample to reflect the increasing popularity of trucks. In principle this different source of information for selecting a sample of used cars and trucks should include all used car and truck purchases whether bought from other owners of used cars, dealers or rental agencies, etc. If the BLS selected a random sample of all used vehicle purchases reported by the CES, the percentage of vehicles selected from the CES sample that were among the top 10 best selling vehicles should be a close match for the share of sales accounted by the top 10 vehicles of all domestically produced and imported vehicles. This is what I expected but, much to my surprise, did not find.

The 1998 sample included 1210 observations (spanning the 1993 to 1998 model years) of which 217 (18%) were among the top 10 new cars and trucks. As mentioned above, light trucks were included in the sample for the first time in 1998. The inclusion of trucks in the sample causes an even larger distortion between the BLS sample of cars and trucks in the top 10 and the share of sales of 10 best selling new cars and trucks over the last five years. In 1998 the top 10 selling cars and trucks (from 1993 to 1998) accounted for 39% of the domestic car and truck production plus imports. Most surprising, the gap between 18% and 39% remained large in spite of the use of the CES to create a new BLS sample of cars and trucks.[ii] Some peculiarities appear when the 1998 sample of cars is scanned. For example, the 1998 sample contains more Corvettes than Camry observations.

Time and budget constraints prevented me from investigating the cause of the unexpected discrepancy in 1998. I have been told that the CES is a sample of all used car transactions and the BLS takes a very small sample of that sample. Perhaps, sampling variation is responsible for the large discrepancies documented above. If this is the reason, then serious thought should be given to increasing the size of the sample. I am not convinced that this is the complete explanation so I remain perplexed by the 1998 results.

This investigator believes the procedures for drawing the sample of cars needs to be reexamined. Throughout the nineteen-nineties the BLS sample of cars has deviated from the population of used cars in the market. Possible reasons for the observed deviations between 1990 and 1997 have been given above. However, the deviation observed in 1998 when the CES sample was drawn remain a puzzle, a puzzle that needs to be solved.

Given the limited alternatives available and the large discrepancies found in this paper, feasible alternative procedures are not easy to recommend. Perhaps the easiest solution, though still imperfect, is for the BLS to select a sample of used cars based on the sales of new cars over the previous six years. While this procedure has some drawbacks, it is easier to implement and appears to be an improvement over the results achieved to date by using either the Runzheimer Report or the CES.

B. Differences Between the Retention Rates of the Top 10 Best Selling New Cars and Less Popular Cars

Could the share differences found throughout the nineties be due to the longer holding periods of buyers of the top ten selling new cars? There is fragmentary evidence that buyers of new imported cars hold them longer before trading them in. In a study of ownership changes for cars and trucks registered in Illinois, Porter and Sattler (1999) calculated the fraction of cars traded in as of December 1994 for owners who bought new 1986 - 1988 model year cars. On average cars bought between 1986 and 1988 would be 7 years old in December 1994. The authors report trade-in data by division of company. For example, the Ford car group represents all cars marketed by the Ford division of the Ford Motor company while the Honda car group would represent all cars marketed by the Honda division, e.g. Accord, Civic, etc. If we select from the Porter-Sattler (P/S hereafter) study, the ten car groups with the lowest fractions traded in, the weighted average fraction of cars traded-in was .454. In other words, only 45% of these cars when they were bought new in the model years 1986-1998 had been traded by December 1994. It turns out all of the ten car groups represented imported cars, e.g. Volvo, VW, Saab, Subaru, Honda, Toyota etc. These ten car groups accounted for only .140 of the total cars in the sample throughout the 1986-1988 model years. Since the fraction of cars traded-in for the sample as a whole was .541, the fraction of cars traded-in for the remaining car groups averaged .555. For 1986-1988 model years, original owners of imported cars retained their cars for longer periods than owners of cars produced by American manufacturers.

While a larger fraction of imported cars were retained by their original owners, this was not true for the best selling cars during the 1986-1988 model years (mostly American cars during this time period) where the difference between the percentage traded-in of the ten largest selling car groups and the other car groups was negligible.

Since 1988, foreign cars have risen in the sales charts with Toyota, Honda, Civic and other imported cars regularly ranked among the top ten cars throughout the nineties. As a consequence, the top ten best selling new cars in the nineties could very well have higher retention rates than other car models because more imported models were in the top ten best selling cars. Could the difference between the market share of the top ten best selling cars in the new car market and the lower fraction that BLS used cars were among the top ten cars be due to the higher retention rates for imported cars?

What fraction of the used car market would the top 10 new cars command if they were held for longer period by their original owners? By making a few assumptions, an estimate of the share that the top selling cars would have of the used market can be derived. Assume that the top 10 best selling new cars in the nineties were traded in as infrequently as the ten car groups with the lowest trade-in fractions during the 1986-1988 model years. This is obviously a generous estimate since some of the top ten best selling cars in the nineties were cars produced by domestic producers that typically have lower retention rates. Between 1990-1997, the top ten best selling new cars accounted for an average of 43.6% of all domestically produced and imported cars. If the retention rates of these cars were the same as the retention rates of the 1986-1988 model year cars with the ten lowest trade-in fractions, then the <u>ratio</u> of the fraction that the top 10 best selling new cars would account for in the used market to their fraction of the new car market is given by

$$\frac{s_1^u}{s_1^n} = \frac{s_1^n t_1}{s_1^n t_1 + (1-s_1^n)t_2} \frac{1}{s_1^n} = \frac{1}{s_1^n + (1-s_1^n)t_2 / t_1}$$

where $\dfrac{s_1^u}{s_1^n}$ is the ratio of share of the used car market that would be accounted for by the top 10 best selling new cars to the share of the new car market accounted for by the top 10 best selling cars and t_2/t_1 (> 1) is the ratio of the fraction traded-in of all cars other than the top 10 best selling cars (t_2) to the fraction traded-in of the top 10 best selling cars (t_1). This equation can be rewritten as

$$\frac{s_1^u}{1-s_1^u} = \frac{t_1}{t_2} \frac{s_1^n}{1-s_1^n}$$

Because $\dfrac{t_1}{t_2}$ is less than one, s_1^u will be less than s_1^n.

The top 10 best selling cars accounted for an average fraction of .436 of the new car imported cars. Inserting these numbers into the equation above yields an estimate for $\frac{s_1^u}{s_1^n}$ = .888.[iv] The market share of the used market held by the top 10 best selling cars in the new market would be lower than their market share of the new market but only by a about 12 % even under the generous assumption that the top 10 cars as a group could match the retention rates of the imports for the model years 1986-1988. Given the top 10's average new car share is .436, the equation would predict their average used car share would be.387. Consequently, the larger mean discrepancy that was found between the mean share of BLS used cars that were among the top 10 best selling new cars and the mean of the actual market share of the top 10 in the new car market cannot be explained by the fact that the top 10 selling new cars are traded in less frequently than all other cars. Something else is causing the large observed discrepancy.

Two caution flags should be waved. The P/S study -- from which estimates of frequency of trade-in data was obtained -- is from a single state, Illinois. How representative is Illinois of the nation is unknown. Second the estimates are based on the trade-in experience in the 1986 to 1988 period. It is unknown whether the frequency with which buyers retain their new cars has changed over time.

V. The Effect of the Source of Used Car Price Data

The greater volatility of used car prices may be spurious in part and depend on the data source used by the BLS. Could the reliance on auction price data contribute to the higher price volatility of used car prices? This section reviews an earlier study that relied on used car price data published in car guides to develop separate new and used car price indices. The study used hedonic techniques to account for price changes caused by changes in the physical characteristics of cars. These hedonic adjusted price indices are compared to the CPI price indices for new and used cars. In the second part of this section, I compare price data taken from Kelley's Blue Book with NADA auction price data to determine if used car price volatility depends on the source of the data.

A. Gordon's New and Used Car Price Index Study

In his study of new and used car prices Gordon (1990) developed new and used car price indices from 1947 to 1983 using prices reported in new and used car price guides. Gordon borrowed a methodology first implemented by Griliches and Ohta (1976). In essence, Gordon estimates a hedonic for used (new) cars while controlling for the effects of selected car physical characteristics and including a time dummy variable to measure an autonomous change in used car prices. In his hedonic regressions he includes weight, length, brake horsepower, age and type of engine. The time dummy measures changes in either the used (new) car price after controlling for the effects of car characteristics listed above. The estimated coefficient for the time dummy is obtained from regressions of successive two-year cross sectional observations. Gordon cautions the limitations of the hedonic approach especially for later years in his study where the more difficult to measure attributes like interior space, trim lines, environmental improvements become more prominent. He also questions the usefulness of car size in any hedonic regression when cars were downsized during the second half of the 1970s, especially in 1977 and 1979.

Gordon's study examines price behavior of four-door sedans manufactured by the then Big 3, Chrysler, Ford and General Motors. Given the time frame of the study, imports were not considered. Figure 2 shows a scatter diagram for P_t/P_{t-1} derived from the CPI used car price index against P_t/P_{t-1} of Gordon's hedonic price index. The correlation coefficient between the two series equals .675 over the entire 1954-1983 period but the correlation coefficient varies a lot from sub-period to sub-period. There is considerable variability in the CPI price ratio especially when the price ratio derived from the hedonic is above 1.

**Figure 2: A Comparison of CPI Used Car Price Ratio With
Gordon's Hedonic Price Ratio**

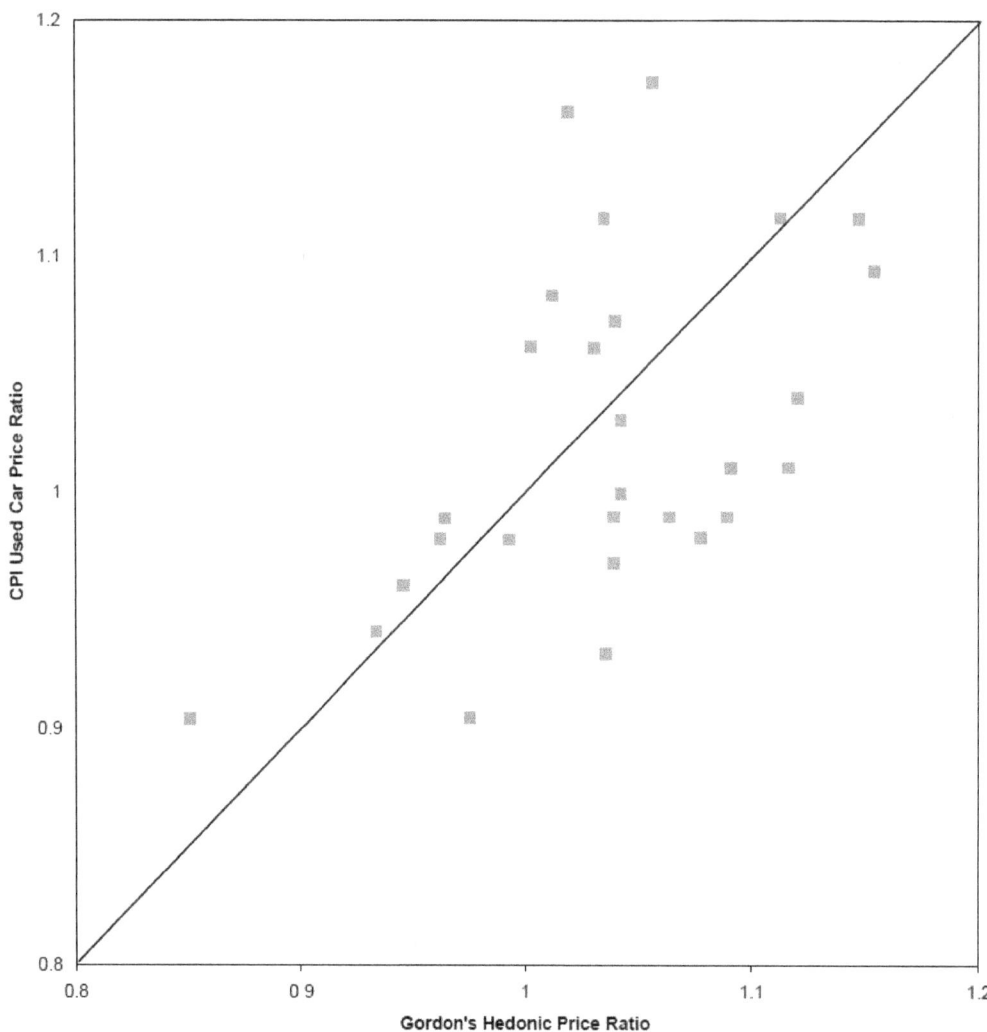

Table 6 shows the mean, standard deviation and the SD/M ratio of P_t/P_{t-1} from 1953 to 1983 and for two sub-periods from 1953 –1974 and from 1975-1983 for the CPI and for the hedonic price indexes. Summary statistics are presented for both new and used cars.

The CPI used car price index grows on average by 1.1 percentage points faster per year than the hedonic index. Here again the failure to adjust the used car price index for quality improvements is the likely cause, especially in the earlier period from 1953 to 1974, and gave an upward bias to the used car price index. As mentioned above, the correlation coefficient between the two price indexes was .675. In the more stable earlier period from 1953-1974 the difference in the mean growth rate was about 3.9 percentage points. In the more volatile period from 1975-1983 the mean growth rates of the two indexes are about the same.

This comparison of the CPI with the hedonic price indices does not suggest that used car price index would display less volatility if the BLS had used a different source for price data <u>and</u> adopted the hedonic methodology. The hedonic used car price index has a larger standard deviation than the CPI in the more volatile period from 1975 to 1983. Even more disturbing is that the correlation coefficient between the two indexes from 1975-1983 drops to only .378. The two indexes move in the opposite directions in 1977 and 1979, two years when American car producers introduced major downsizing programs. The lower correlation coefficient suggests that the regression coefficients for weight, engine size, etc., in the hedonic regression equations were not that stable in a period of major downsizing of cars.[v]

Gordon's pioneering study is a useful investigation. It represents a rare effort to use non-CPI price data to construct new and used car price indexes. Gordon's derived price indexes are different from the CPI price indices for new or used cars in two ways. First, the data source is different and second the methodology for correcting for quality change is different. It is apparent that Gordon's derived new and used car price indices leave much to be desired especially over the 1975–1983 period. Given currently available price and car characteristics data, his results raise doubts that a hedonic approach will necessarily reduce the volatility of used car prices compared to the methods currently used to calculate the used car component of the CPI, especially during periods of rapid changes in product offerings.

B. <u>Comparing the Mean Growth and Volatility of Kelley's Prices with NADA Prices</u>

When calculating the used car price index, the CPI starts with the raw auction prices as reported in the NADA Guide Book. These data are collected from numerous dealer auctions held throughout the country. The auction prices resemble wholesale prices since they are prices paid by dealers for cars that are subsequently resold to the final consumer after any reconditioning. Other secondary sources of used car price information exist. As mentioned above, a number of commercial used car price guides have published price data for many years. Some guides report the prices that dealers pay for used cars and retail used car prices. One such guide is Kelley's Blue Book. Kelley's publishes trade-in prices, i.e., the price that a dealer would pay for a trade-in, and retail prices for used cars four times a year. How much "smoothing" of the price data is done by Kelley's or by the NADA prior to publication is unknown but is likely both sources smooth data by eliminating extreme price observations and, possibly, include their prior assessments of movements in car prices. As the 1999 Blue Book notes, "This guide book represents the opinion of the staff and management of Kelley Blue Book and is arrived at after careful study of information we deem reliable."(Blue Book)

For this paper, a pilot project was conducted whose purpose is to determine if the source of the price data affects the mean price change and price volatility. NADA price (auction) data were compared with Kelley's <u>trade-in</u> (the price that dealers pay for a car) used car price data. Kelley's trade-in price was used because it, rather than the retail price, comes closest to the NADA auction price. The initial step in this exercise takes NADA's list of outlets (auctions) starting with the 1990 sample and selects only those outlets that reported prices for the same car (model) in adjacent years. This procedure assures that the price quotations in successive years are for the same model at the same auction location. While this matching procedure assures a degree of comparability between the price observations for successive years, the procedure cannot guarantee that the two cars are identical, e.g., mileage might be different.

A 20 percent sample was selected of the cars that satisfy this requirement in each year beginning with the 1990 sample and continuing through to the 1997 sample. In years when the sample was rotated (changed), it was not possible to match cars because prices were not available in both years, e.g., 1993-1994. For each NADA car that was included in the 20 percent sample, the published Kelley's price for a base car was adjusted for option package of the NADA car. Currently, Kelley's assigns cars to one of 6 option package categories. Each category has a different set of options. Cars assigned by Kelley's to class 1 are higher priced cars where most options are standard while cars assigned to category 6 are lower priced cars where few options are standard. A 20 percent sample of cars was selected because matching the Kelley's car options with the BLS car options and then adjusting the Kelley's prices for options is tedious and time consuming. A more comprehensive investigation would require more time and resources.

Whenever Kelley's package of options differed from the package on the NADA car, e.g., the NADA car had a larger or smaller engine, the Kelley's price was adjusted based on Kelley's estimates of the retail prices for the more popular options. By following this procedure, the price that a dealer would pay for a trade-in was estimated based on information provided by Kelley's for a car similarly equipped as the NADA car. While the information supplied by Kelley's can be used to adjust the Kelley's prices, not all options are priced so some differences between the NADA and the Kelley's price data remain. Best effort was made to identify trim lines and to compare prices for the same trim line of car. A more important difference between the NADA and the Kelley car is that the mileage of the Kelley car is suppose to be for a car with a specified mileage range that depends on the age of car. On the other hand, the mileage of the NADA cars is unknown but is likely to be higher since these are traded-ins by rental car companies, etc. While a dedicated effort was made to assure comparability between the NADA and Kelley's cars, some differences undoubtedly remain.

Once the prices have been derived for the similarly equipped cars, the mean growth and the standard deviation of each cross section of cars can be calculated for each year and for each price source. The percentage price changes between adjacent years can also be calculated first using NADA prices and then Kelley's estimates of the prices that dealers pay. The mean and standard deviation of the percentage change in price between adjacent years can be calculated.

Table 7 shows the cross sectional mean, standard deviation, and the ratio of the standard deviation to the mean of prices starting with the adjacent years 1990-91. In the 1990 and 1991 comparison the mean 1990 NADA used car price is $7,774 while the mean of the Kelley's prices is $8,094 for the 49 used cars included in the 20% sample. In 1991 the mean NADA price is $8,032 while the mean Kelley's price is $8,148. I had expected Kelley's mean price to be higher than NADA mean price in all years since I expected the average mileage of the NADA (rental) cars would be higher and/or that the NADA cars are in poorer condition. On the other hand, the cars traded in by rental car companies may have been better maintained than the cars traded in by individuals. Surprisingly, the mean NADA price exceeds the mean Kelly's price in eight of the twelve years.

NADA mean price increased by 3.3% between 1990 and 1991 while Kelley's mean price increased by only 0.7%. This pattern of a more rapid growth in NADA prices is observed in many of the adjacent year comparisons. Looking at the results for the six paired years indicates the percentage change (in absolute value) in the mean price is smaller for Kelley's prices in 5 of the 6 comparisons (the exception is 95-96). It appears that Kelley's mean prices have been more stable over time than NADA prices. The NADA prices appear to catch up and then surpass Kelley's prices between 1990 and 1995 after which Kelley's prices are abruptly adjusted upward in 1996. By 1997 there is only a small difference between the mean prices.

The last two columns of Table 7 compare the cross-sectional variability of the two price sources in adjacent years. In the 1990-1991 comparison, Kelley's prices have smaller standard deviations and lower SD/M ratios. Looking at all twelve cross sections, Kelley's prices have smaller standard deviations in 10 of the 12 years and smaller SD/M ratios in 8 of the 12 cases. So, Kelley's prices display greater absolute and relative cross sectional stability than NADA prices.

Table 8 compares the times-series variability in NADA and Kelley's prices. The mean percentage change, standard deviation and the standard deviation divided by the mean percentage change are shown for both price sources for successive years. The latter measure has less meaning in the time series comparisons whenever the mean percentage price change is close to zero. Between 1990 and 1991, the mean percentage price change (PPC) equals 3.73% for NADA prices and is 1.16% for Kelley's prices. The standard deviation is 3.41% for NADA prices and 2.39% for Kelley's prices. However, the standard deviation relative to the mean percentage price change is higher for Kelley's prices -- .915 versus 2.060 because the mean percentage price change for Kelley's prices is so low. The last column shows the simple correlation of the 1990-1991 percentage price change between Kelley's and NADA was only .176.

Looking at all six paired years, the standard deviation of the individual percentage price changes is smaller for Kelley's prices in all 6 comparisons. These results suggest that the PPC's of Kelley's prices are less volatile. NADA prices are more variable between adjacent years. Turning to the simple correlation coefficients between the PPC's of Kelley's and NADA prices, they are quite variable ranging from a low of .176 for the price changes between 1990-1991 to a high of .759 for price changes between 1992-1993. The average correlation coefficient is only .423. I had expected to observe reasonably high coefficients between the percentage price changes from the two sources. Obviously, the two data sources often disagree with respect to the percentage price changes.

This pilot project was limited in scope because of time and data constraints. Consequently, it is perhaps wise not to make too much of the results. Clearly, more study is needed before a final assessment can be reached. What does seem clear is that the cross sectional and time series volatility of Kelley's prices appears smaller. So, there is some evidence that the source of the price information contributes to the observed "excess" volatility of used car prices. There is a clear hint in these results that price volatility might be lower if the BLS used a different price source.

An expanded project that included more years would have to be completed before a definitive assessment can be reached. Such a project could determine if used car price volatility could be reduced by even more if the BLS used a weighted average of NADA and Kelley's prices. The low correlation between NADA and Kelley's price changes suggest that measured volatility would be lower if a weighted average of the price changes was adopted. In addition, such an expanded study should investigate quarterly used car percentage price changes to determine if similar results are found when the quarterly Kelley's prices are compared to the NADA prices. Another area to investigate is whether the inclusion of still other secondary sources might reduce volatility by even more.

VI. Testing the Quality Adjustment Assumption

The used car price index measures the mean price change of used cars after adjusting used car prices for any year to year quality change. Currently, the BLS adjusts used car prices for quality change by using the new car quality adjustment factor (percentage), as originally supplied to the BLS by manufacturers but modified by the BLS, to adjust used cars prices for any quality change as manufacturers introduce improved cars. For used cars, BLS applies this same new car quality adjustment factor as the car ages. For example, if quality improvements raise the cost of producing a new car by 1% from the previous year's model, the BLS assumes that the used car price of the model will also be higher by 1% from the previous year's model because of the quality improvements as the car ages. In other words, this quality adjustment procedure assumes that the quality adjustment percentage is independent of the age of the car.

Two assumptions of the BLS quality change adjustment can be tested. First, prices quoted in the used car market reflect the value consumers place on quality change. Used car prices for a given model in successive years can be used to determine if the measured percentage quality factor has a significant effect on used car prices. Second, the price of a used car of a given age that had a quality change of k% when new can be compared to the price of the previous year's model (of the same age) that does not have the k% added quality improvements. For example, assume that a new car introduced at the end of year t-2 had a k% quality improvement factor when new. At the end of year t this car is two years old and its used car price is P_t^2. This price can be expected to exceed the used car price of two-year-old car of the same model in year t-1, P_{t-1}^2, if the used car market values the k% quality improvement either partially or fully. Similarly, in the next year the original car will be three years old and its price P_{t+1}^3 can be expected to exceed the price of a three-year-old car in year t P_t^3 if the k% quality improvement is valued in the used car market. By similar reasoning, the prices of similar aged cars in successive years can be compared as the same two cars age through time.

A regression test of the independence hypothesis can be made by regressing the price ratio in successive years for a given age of car on the observed quality adjustment factor and dummy variables for the age of car and for year effects. Such a regression would involve a pooled cross sectional- time series analysis. Regression estimates are provided for the following regression equation

$(P_t^i / P_{t-1}^i - 1)100$

$$= (a_0 + a_3 A_3 + a_4 A_4 + a_5 A_5 + a_6 A_6)(100 + Q_t^i) + b_1 D_{91} + b_2 D_{92} + b_3 D_{93} + b_4 D_{94} + b_5 D_{95} \ldots \ldots$$

where the subscript for model is suppressed. A is a dummy variable that equals one if the car is two years old or three years old, etc. as the case may be and D is dummy variable equal to 1 if the year is 1991 etc., as the case may be. Q_t^i denotes the quality adjustment factor for the car when new. The dependent variable is the percentage price change of a model of age i in year t compared to the price of the same model and same age car in year t − 1. The percentage price change is assumed to be proportional to 100 + the percentage quality improvement factor. If the coefficient a_0 equals 1, the percentage price ratio increases by the percentage quality improvement factor. If it is zero, the used car market equation includes year effects that would account for stronger or weaker years for the used car market that would cause prices to rise or fall relative to the previous year.

Before looking at the regression results, it is instructive to look at some summary measures. A little less than eighty-four percent of the observations are for two and three year old cars. So, most of the observations are for younger used cars. The mean of the percentage price change for NADA prices is 104.0 and the standard deviation is 8.20. The mean of the percentage quality improvement factor is 100.9 but the standard deviation is only 1.40. These summary statistics show that there is considerably more variability in the percentage price ratio than in the quality improvement factor. Hence, the percentage improvement factor is not likely to be an important factor in explaining the percentage price change. On the other hand, the results of the previous section suggest that year effects will be important determinants of the percentage price change.

Columns 1 and 2 of Table 9 confirm these conjectures. Regression results for NADA prices are in column 1 while column 2 show results for Kelley's prices. In both regression equations the year effects dominate the effects of quality and age. After controlling for year effects, the percentage quality factor is not even a significant determinant of the percentage price ratio. Virtually all of the age interaction variables are insignificant as well. Hence, the used car market appears to completely disregard the percentage quality adjustment factor in establishing used car prices. These are interesting and in some ways surprising results and cast some doubt on the BLS use of the quality improvement factor to adjust used car prices for quality change.

V. Summary and Conclusions

This paper has reexamined the used car price index to identify some of its strengths and weaknesses with the goal of suggesting some improvements. Among the findings are

- The failure to adjust used car prices for quality change between 1952 and 1987 helps explain why the used car price index rose more rapidly than the new car price index. Apparently, the quality improvement procedures adopted by the BLS in 1987 effectively eliminated the discrepancy between the mean of new and used car percentage price changes.
- Used car prices are among the more volatile in the CPI. The source of the price data used by the BLS appears to contribute to the excess volatility of the used car price index. Preliminary evidence indicates that Kelley's prices are less volatile than NADA prices so that the used car price index would show less volatility if prices were based on Kelley's than NADA. Even if a better price data source is found, used car prices may still be more volatile. Another explanation for the volatility of used car prices is based on real factors, e.g., the supply curve is less elastic for used than new

better to rely on the sales experience of new cars over the last six years to draw the sample.

- The under sampling of more popular cars is not due to buyers of the more popular cars being held longer by the original owners.
- The BLS adjustment of used car prices for quality improvement assumes that its measure of quality improvements affects used car prices and has the same percentage effect independent of the age of car. Regression results casts some doubt on the appropriateness of the quality adjustment since the percentage quality improvement variable is not a significant determinant of the percentage price change between models one year apart.

Bibliography

Gordon, Robert, The Measurement of Durable Goods Prices, National Bureau of Economic Research, University of Chicago Press,1990.

Ohta,Makoto and Zvi Griliches, "Automobile Prices Revisited: Extensions on the Hedonic Hypothesis," Household Production and Consumption, ed. N. E.Terleckyj, New York, National Bureau of Economic Research, 1976, 325-90.

Kellar, Jeffrey, "New Methodology Reduces Importance of Used Cars in the Revised CPI," Monthly Labor Review, December 1988, 34-36.

Kelley Blue Book, Used Car Guide, January-June 2000, No. 1.

Pashigian, B. Peter, Brian Bowen and Eric Gould, "Fashion, Styling and the Within Season Decline in Automobile Prices," Journal of Law and Economics, October 1995, 281-310.

Porter, Robert H. and Peter Sattler, "Patterns of Trade In The Market For Used Durables: Theory and Evidence," National Bureau of Economic Research, Inc., Working Paper 7149, May 1999.

Stewart, Kenneth J. and Stephen B Reed, "Consumer Price Index Research Series Using Current Methods, 1978-98" Monthly Labor Review, June 1999, 29-38.

Table 1: Volatility of P_t/P_{t-1} for Selected Products and Sectors, Annual Data						
	New Vehicles, 1955-98	Used Vehicles, 1955-98	Energy, 1957-98	Food, 1955-98	Consumer Price Index (CPI), 1955-98	CPI excluding Energy, Food, Shelter and Used Cars, 1967-98
1. Mean (M)	1.026	1.047	1.042	1.042	1.043	1.048
2. Standard Deviation (SD)	.0287	.0671	.0823	.0345	.0301	.0120
3. SD/Mean	.0280	.0641	.0790	.0331	.0289	.0188
4. SD/Mean of Product Relative to SD/Mean of Used Vehicles	.44	1.00	1.23	.52	.45	.29

Table 2: Volatility of P_t/P_{t-1} for Selected Sub-Periods, Annual Data						
	New Vehicles	Used Vehicles	Energy	Food	Consumer Price Index (CPI)	CPI excluding Energy, Food, Shelter and Used Cars
1955 - 1975						
1. Mean	1.017	1.041	1.042	1.039	1.037	1.053
2. Standard Deviation	.0316	.0678	.0680	.0413	.0276	.0203
3. SD/Mean	.0311	.0651	.0653	.0397	.0266	.0193
4. SD/Mean Relative to SD/Mean of Used Cars	.48	1.00	1.003	.61	.41	.30
1976 -1998						
1. Mean	1.035	1.053	1.042	1.045	1.049	1.046
2. Standard Deviation	.0227	.0675	.0945	.0273	.0318	.0195
3. SD/Mean	.0219	.0641	.0907	.0261	.0303	.0187
4. SD/Mean of Product Relative to SD/Mean of Used Cars	.34	1.00	1.42	.41	.47	.29
1989-1998						
1. Mean	1.021	1.026	1.015	1.031	1.033	1.034
2. Standard Deviation	.0135	.0466	.0424	.0154	.0119	.0125
3. SD/Mean	.0133	.0454	.0418	.0149	.0115	.0121
4. SD/Mean of Product Relative to SD/Mean of Used Cars	.29	1.00	.92	.33	.25	.27

Table 3: Seasonal Volatility of Monthly Price Index, (non-seasonally adjusted to seasonally adjusted price)						
	New Vehicles	Used Vehicles	Energy	Food	Consumer Price Index (CPI)	CPI excluding Energy, Food, Shelter and Used Cars
1955-1998						
1. Mean	1.000	1.000	1.001	.999	1.000	1.000
2. Standard Deviation	.0116	.0187	.0115	.0039	.0016	.0022
3. SD/Mean	.0116	.0187	.0115	.0039	.0016	.0022
4. SD/Mean of Product Relative to SD/Mean of Used Cars	.62	1.00	.61	.21	.09	.12

Table 4: Volatility of Monthly Prices (MP$_t$/MP$_{t-1}$ for Seasonally Adjusted Monthly Prices)						
	New Vehicles	Used Vehicles	Energy	Food	Consumer Price Index (CPI)	CPI excluding Energy, Food, Shelter and Used Cars
1955-1998						
1. Mean	.220	.398	.319	.336	.345	.391
2. Standard Deviation	.7676	1.4410	1.2643	.5468	.3044	.2146
3. SD/Mean	3.4868	3.3614	3.9659	1.6252	.8828	.5488
4. SD/Mean Relative of Product to SD/Mean of Used Cars	1.04	1.00	1.18	.48	.26	.16
1989-1998						
1. Mean	.162	.142	.096	.242	.256	.259
2. Standard Deviation	.215	.618	1.403	.282	.169	.147
3. SD/Mean	1.32	4.36	14.67	1.16	.66	.57
4. SD/Mean Relative of Product to SD/Mean of Used Cars	.30	1.00	3.36	.27	.15	.13

Table 5: How Representativeness Is the BLS Used Car Sample?									
	1990	1991	1992	1993	1994	1995	1996	1997	1998 *
1. Number of BLS Models Among Top 10 Best Selling Cars over the last five years	150	182	192	230	269	239	231	280	217
2. Total Models in BLS Sample	746	697	719	735	979	961	987	1003	1210
3. Percentage of BLS cars in Top 10 over the last five years	20%	26%	27%	31%	27%	25%	23%	28%	18%
4. Combined Market Share Percentage of Top 10 Domestic & Imported Cars of Total Domestically Produced Sales	58	77	82	83	60	81	60	49	50
5. Combined Market Share Percentage of Top 10 Domestic and Imported Cars of Total Domestically Produced plus Imported Cars	37	44	47	48	41	51	43	38	39
6. Combined Market Share Percentage of Top 10 Domestic and Imported Cars of Total Domestically Produced Cars and Light Trucks and Imports.	23	26	26	26	23	26	23	21	21

Includes top 10 cars and trucks

Table 6: P_t/P_{t-1} for CPI and Hedonic Used and New Car Price Indexes				
Period	Used Cars		New Cars	
	CPI	Hedonic	CPI	Hedonic
1. 1953 –1983				
a. Mean	1.048	1.037	1.026	1.037
b. Standard Deviation	.080	.086	.035	.066
c. Correlation Coefficient	.675		.648	
2. 1953-1974				
a. Mean	1.043	1.004	1.014	1.016
b. Standard Deviation	.064	.064	.031	.047
c. Correlation Coefficient	.661		.610	
3. 1975-1983				
a. Mean	1.109	1.105	1.060	1.097
b. Standard Deviation	.070	.085	.020	.078
c. Correlation Coefficient	.378		.263	

Table 7: Mean, Standard Deviation and SD/M of Prices Dealers Pay for Used Cars – NADA Versus Kelley's Prices						
Year	Mean Price (M)		Standard Deviation of Prices (SD)		Standard Deviation /Mean Price (SD/M)	
	NADA	Kelley's	NADA	Kelley's	NADA	Kelley's
1. 1990, N = 49	$7,774	$8,094	$3,854	$3,690	.496	.456
1991, N = 49	8,032	8148	3,821	3,581	.476	.439
% change in Mean Price (90-91)	3.3	0.7				
2. 1991, N = 58	8,119	8,176	2,615	2,555	.322	.313
1992, N = 58	8,801	8,529	2,786	2,713	.316	.318
% change in Mean Price (91-92)	8.4	4.3				
3. 1992, N = 54	8,481	8,201	2,803	2,610	.330	.318
1993, N = 54	9,369	9,039	3,128	2,811	.334	.311
% change in Mean Price (92-93)	10.5	10.2				
1993-1994	na	na	na	na	na	na
4. 1994, N = 25	9,905	9,332	4,080	3,505	.429	.376
1995, N = 25	10,226	9,560	3,832	3,450	.375	.361
% change in Mean Price (94-95)	7.6	2.4				
5. 1995, N = 74	10,361	9,741	3,498	3,200	.338	.328
1996, N = 74	10,516	10,235	3,476	3,396	.331	.332
% change in Mean Price (95-96)	1.9	5.1				
6. 1996, N =41	10,953	10,549	3,688	3,670	.337	.348
1997, N= 41	10,460	10,483	3,581	3,597	.342	.343
% change in Mean Price (96-97)	-4.5	-1.0				
1997-1998	na	na	na	na	na	na

Table 8: Volatility in the Percentage Price Change of NADA and Kelley's Used Car Prices			
	Mean (M) , Standard Deviation (SD) of Percentage Price Change and M/SD		Correlation of Percentage Price Change Between NADA and Kelley's
Year	NADA (1)	Kelley's (2)	
1990-1991	M = 3.73 SD = 3.41 SD/M = .915	1.16 2.39 2.06	.176
1991-1992	8.55 5.30 .62	4.22 4.87 1.15	.432
1992-1993	10.63 7.63 .718	10.44 5.26 .504	.759
1993-1994	na	na	na
1994-1995	10.70 10.78 1.01	2.89 4.05 1.40	.274
1995-96	1.78 4.04 2.27	5.09 3.85 .76	.341
1996-97	-4.63 6.16 -1.33	-.43 3.37 -7.80	.557
1997-98	na	na	na

Table 9: Effect of Quality Change, Age of Car and Year on Percentage Price Change		
	NADA Prices	Kelley's Prices
Variable	(1)	(2)
Percentage Quality Change (PQC)	-.025 (-.1)	-.031 (-.2)
PQC*Three Years Old	-.003 (-.3)	-.004 (1.3)
PQC*Four Years Old	-.011 (-.8)	.003 (.4)
PQC*Five Years Old	.043 (2.8)	.007 (.7)
PQC*Six Years Old	.056 (-2.6)	.023 (1.5)
1991	106.3 (4.4)	104.3 (6.3)
1992	111.1 (4.6)	107.5 (6.5)
1993	113.2 (4.7)	113.7 (6.8)
1995	112.5 (4.6)	105.9 (6.4)
1996	104.0 (4.3)	108.2 (6.5)
1997	97.7 (4.0)	102.7 (6.2)
R2 (adjusted)	.997	.999
Root MSE	5.93	4.06

t statistics in brackets

_____

Footnotes

*Helpful comments and suggestions were received from John S. Greenlees, Tim Lafleur and Dennis Fixler. Bonifacius Pasaribu served ably as my research assistant. This study was supported by the Bureau of Labor Statistics and by the Lynde and Harry Bradley, and the Sarah Scaife Foundations through grants to the George J. Stigler Center for the Study of the Economy and the State, the University of Chicago.

[i] In personal correspondence John S. Greenlees notes that Stuart and Reed (Monthly Labor Review) constructed a revised CPI-U series back to 1978 using current CPI methodology. In unpublished work the authors find their adjustments to the used car price index for quality improvements would have lowered the index by 0.6 percentage point per year between 1978 and 1986.

[ii] If the 1998 sample is limited to just cars, 30% of the BLS cars account are in the top 10 while the top 10 cars account for 39% of all domestically produced and imported cars. If the sample is restricted to light trucks, 38% of the BLS trucks were in the top 10 selling light trucks while the top ten selling new light trucks represented 53% of all the light trucks sold.

[iii] The formula can be modified to account for differences in the frequency of trades of the car given that the original owner sells the car.

[iv] The estimate of the fraction of non- Top10 cars that are traded in is derived from the equation

$$.140(.454) + .860t_2 = .541$$

[v] For new cars, the hedonic price index exhibits more variability over the whole period and grows faster by 1.1 percentage points with much of the difference occurring in the 1975-1983 period. Unlike used cars, the difference between the mean growth rates for new cars is modest from 1953-1974 suggesting the CPI adjustments for quality changes of new cars were more accurate than for used cars. As with used cars, the correlation between the CPI and hedonic indices falls drastically to only .263 in the 1975-1983 period. As with used cars, the hedonic index has a larger standard deviation over this more volatile interval.